La Vie Parisienne

HORROR STORY
The monster

La Vie Parisienne

VICTOR ARWAS

PAPADAKIS

First published in Great Britain in 2010 by
Papadakis Publisher

PAPADAKIS

An imprint of New Architecture Group Limited

HEAD OFFICE: Kimber Studio, Winterbourne, Berkshire, RG20 8AN
DESIGN STUDIO & RETAIL: 11 Shepherd Market, Mayfair, London, W1J 7PG

Tel. +44 (0) 1635 24 88 33
Fax. +44 (0) 1635 24 85 95
info@papadakis.net
www.papadakis.net

Translated from the French by Victor Arwas

Publishing Director: Alexandra Papadakis
Design Director: Aldo Sampieri
Design by: Shirlynn Chui
Editor: Sheila de Vallée
Editorial Assistant: Sarah Roberts

ISBN 978 1 901092 653

A CIP catalogue of this book is available from the British Library

Printed and bound in China

Contents

"Listen, Josephine. A woman must always be her own mistress to avoid being someone else's."

n 1833 Edouard Charton founded the first popular illustrated magazine in Paris, *Le Magazin pittoresque*, inspired by the English publication, *The Penny Magazine*.

It was followed by several others: some, like *Le Frou-Frou*, were basically humorous, issue after issue exclusively of drawn cartoons with a snappy line of text, although it later diversified with an occasional short story. Others, like *La Chronique Parisienne* or *Le Journal amusant* mixed humour with informal discussions of popular or fashionable events. *Le Courrier Français* was more pointed, with weekly cartoons lampooning or satirising current events and prominent politicians, writers and personalities, its humour often cruelly sarcastic. Few lasted more than a few short years as new publications vied for attention.

La Vie Parisienne attempted a fresh mix of humorous cartoons, short stories, sharp little tales of fashion-folk, up-to-the-minute gossip about prominent persons whose names are almost never fully spelled out or who are given pseudonyms; columns of aphorisms on such subjects as marriage ("Marriage is the only really painful operation for which no anaesthetic is allowed," or "Marriage is the end for the man and the beginning for the woman") and love ("Licentiousness is the spice of love," or "Without jealousy even the most violent passions would not last a week"); much fashion-orientated sophisticated banter set out as pages of dialogue; and acid comments about all and sundry, music, art, the theatre, the races, sports, the stock exchange. Somewhat surprisingly, the mixture took. Founded in 1863, Parisians bought it in sufficient numbers week after week to ensure its survival for over a century.

The turn of the century and the first three decades of the twentieth century witnessed an astonishing continuity of success for the magazine, whose light-hearted banter appealed to the more sophisticated in the roaring twenties, then comforted and cheered the new poor in the Depression years of the thirties.

At least part of its success was due to its choice of illustrators and their subjects. It was a cosmopolitan magnet for artists of the most diverse origins. The leader of the pack was Raphaël Kirchner, master of the expressively naughty temptress with the innocent face. Born in 1876 in Vienna, he moved to Paris, where he exhibited at the Salons of the Société des Artistes Français. He supplied a number of magazines with illustrations, but his longest collaboration was with *La Vie Parisienne*.

The arrival of the twentieth century transformed people's expectations, and the magazine was there to fuel their increasing interest in sophistication, in fashion, in the whole paraphernalia of ladies' hats, shoes, gloves and their designers. Kirchner produced a stream of deliciously appealing young women, nude or nearly so, about to lose a covering garment, fully dressed under an open umbrella in the rain, skirt pulled up to avoid splashes, affording us a glimpse of an elegant leg, involved in some sporting activity or just trying on a new hat. Whatever she was doing the Kirchner girl was always elegant, always graceful. He also painted some highly erotic, though never explicit, images for discreet collectors as well as large genre pictures such as mermaids, portraits and caricatural theatrical images, which he exhibited. As his fame grew, his images were reproduced as postcards, which were sold in enormous quantities. It was an era in which people communicated with short scrawled messages on picture postcards. Amazingly popular when they first came out, these coloured postcards are still highly collectible and so sought after all over the world.

When the First World War broke out in 1914 Kirchner sailed to the United States, where his fame had preceded him. He died in New York in 1917, aged forty-one.

Kirchner was the quintessential *La Vie Parisienne* illustrator of the first two decades of the twentieth century, but other illustrators each had his or her characteristic individual style. Umberto Brunelleschi, an Italian theatrical set and costume designer also supplied several other French magazines with drawings, including *Le Rire*, *L'Assiette au Beurre*, *Frou Frou*, *Le Journal des Dames et des Modes* and the *Gazette du Bon Ton*. His watercolours are sumptuous riots of colour: exotic Japanese interiors, Venetian masks, eighteenth century costumes or beautiful women in turbans and swirling robes. His Oriental inclination even extended in

Raphaël Kirchner

"The sky is radiant, the scent of the roses is
sublime, life is wonderful…Forget about your
husband. It's not his fault he's unfaithful, he's
left-handed!"

his early drawings to signing himself 'Aroun-al-Rascid' (Haroun al Rachid). He was later to become a distinguished book illustrator.

Another Italian, Enrico Sacchetti, worked as an illustrator, cartoonist and painter in Florence, Milan and Buenos Aires before his arrival in Paris in 1912, when he supplied *La Vie Parisienne* with drawings for over two years. He was totally committed in these drawings to fashion: he depicts his *donnine*, his little ladies, in the most spectacular clothes of the time, every line and curve accurate yet stylized, the figures not just posing, but 'modelling' in contemporary parlance. His book of fashion plates, *Robes et Femmes* was published in 1913.

Jacques Nam, on the other hand, was a feline-obsessive. Whatever the subject of his drawing, at least one cat makes its appearance, sleek, domesticated or feral, regal and dangerous. He was later to abandon the human figure almost completely to concentrate on his beloved cats, painted in oils or lacquered on panels.

Gerda Wegener was one of the few women illustrators. Born in Copenhagen, where she studied at the Fine Arts Academy, she moved to Paris in 1912. Her watercolours were designed to evoke an erotic frisson in the viewer. Some have a suggestively lesbian approach, others a touch of sado-masochism, but even the most anodyne show a sophisticated, world-weary cynicism. Her private life, too, was quite colourful, including marriage to the Danish landscape painter Einar Wegener, who became the first surgically transformed male-to-female transexual.

Charles Martin developed a pure stylisation that was to become an essential component of Art Deco illustration, and he too produced several luxurious publications. Bernard Boutet de Monvel satirised every aspect of Parisian snobbishness. Joseph Hémard, Léonce Burret, Markous depicted everyday events with humour, while R. de la Nézière concentrated on sporting events. Earlier generations of the magazine had been illustrated by such leading artists as Ferdinand Bac, Alfred Robida, Caran

d'Ache, Luc Métivet, Capiello, Jean Veber and Forain. Their successors in the first decades of the twentieth century also included René Préjelan, Fabiano and Léonnec.

Although the illustrators won the magazine much of its success, the writers were equally distinguished in the history of French literature. Many contributions were printed anonymously or under pseudonyms, but others were named or later identified. Ludovic Halévy contributed several short stories and wrote many of the magazine's comments and much of its gossip; together with Henri Meilhac, another regular contributor, they were to form a formidable duo of playwrights and librettists. Théodore de Banville, Paul Bourget, Francis de Miomandre, Abel Hermant, Franc-Nohain and Maurice Donnay, later successful novelists, honed their skills writing for it. Colette contributed several tales, including *La Vagabonde*, *L'Entrave*, and *Vrilles de la Vigne*; while another woman, Sibylle Aimée Marie Antoinette Gabrielle Riqueti de Mirabeau, the last of her illustrious family, who sent her contributions under the pseudonym 'Gyp' liked it so much that all her subsequent writings were published under that name. Maurice Dekobra, later a phenomenally popular romantic novelist (he wrote *The Madonna of the Sleeping Cars*), wrote regular sharply humorous items, while Romain Coolus the playwright contributed many pages entirely in dialogue form. Many poets supplied verse of varying lengths as well as prose, the most distinguished being undoubtedly Baudelaire.

'Celebrities' were at the heart of much of the gossip. Political intrigues, revelations and scandals were eagerly pursued. The years, alas, have been unkind to politicians, most of whom are now decently forgotten, their names holding less meaning than those of minor Pharaohs of ancient Egypt, so most of their intrigues and scandals have as much relevance today as would their laundry lists. More durable is the gossip about performers, actors, singers, dancers and the fascinating demi-mondaines, the denizens of that worldly half-world perched precariously between fame and notoriety, stage and bedroom.

"The Ballets Russes is back," proclaimed one entry, "and once again scored a great success. The other evening over supper Mr. Serge de Diaghilev, who organises all those events, was talking about some aspects of the divine Nijinsky, speaking with that delicious Russian accent which it is impossible to transcribe: 'Ah! Nijinsky, what an admirable artist!...and so conscientious!...At night he

HOW THEY READ THE CLASSICS

1. The lyrical eloquence of Chateaubriand

2. The erotic chronicles of Brantôme

3. The voluptuous poetry of Alfred de Musset

4. The Fables of La Fontaine

5. The romantic poems of Lord Byron

6. The superhuman prose of Nietzsche

leaps out of bed…runs to the mirror and, totally naked, tries out new poses…It's a marvellous sight!... But afterwards when he gets back into bed his feet are so cold…'"

Another entry refers to the great Symbolist poet and playwright: "Mr. Maurice Maeterlinck, who has returned to Paris to direct the latest rehearsals of his play *Marie-Magdeleine* with his wife Mme Georgette Leblanc in the leading role, is a fervent admirer of boxing. But while others (…) prefer to see champions beating each other up, Mr Maeterlinck is a regular participant: in Nice he took daily boxing lessons, so that the 'swings,' the 'cross' and the 'uppercut' hold no secrets for him. This passion worries Mme Georgette Leblanc who is always fearful that her husband might emerge from one of his training sessions with a broken nose or shattered teeth. But the author of

A glass of claret to pass the time while waiting for the sweetmeats

the *Blue Bird* disdains such childish apprehensions, and when he has successfully essayed a combination, tells his wife: 'Ah! That was a great punch. Isn't it just as beautiful as a five-act drama!'"

Another entry, the lady unnamed but immediately identifiable by the magazine's eagle-eyed readers began: "She is one of our prettiest actresses, and is the subject of much gossip, firstly because she was the lover of an ephemeral little king, then because she created a zoological dance number which had its moment of fame. According to reporters and producers, she is the woman with the biggest collection of jewellery, so her little friends have some excuse for a little jealousy. One of them, who graduated brilliantly from the music-hall to the legitimate theatre and now manifests some vaguely literary aspirations, organised a little joke to 'rag' her, as she says in her not-quite-academic style. Each time the creator of the 'grizzly bear' entered a restaurant, Mademoiselle Mistinguett would immediately ask the gypsy band to play that popular air 'The woman with the jewels'… To be constantly welcomed with that inevitable tune in the way the President of the Republic is welcomed with the Marseillaise has become so unbearable for the actress that she has given up dining out."

The 'pretty actress' was one of the magnificent *grandes horizontales*, the Spanish dancer Caroline Otero, known as La Belle Otero and her "ephemeral little king" was a truly whopping understatement: in the course of her erotically careering career she had affairs with King Edward VII of Great Britain, the Kings of Serbia and Spain, the Kaiser, Czar Nicholas II, Grand Dukes Peter and Nicholas, the Duke of Westminster and the Italian poet Gabriele d'Annunzio. Her collection of jewellery was truly enormous. It included a bolero studded with diamonds and gem stones. She had to be accompanied by four armed guards whenever she wore it.

La Vie Parisienne was a magical name that proclaimed itself proudly as the masthead of a way of life in which frivolity, wit and satire were as important and as relevant as literary and political intellectualism. And when Suzy Solidor, one of the greatest French chanteuses whose gravelly voice seduced both men and women decided to open her own nightclub in Paris in the nineteen thirties, she named it, inevitably, *La Vie Parisienne.*

At
the
Seaside

THE LATEST BATHING SUITS

1. For a Russian dancer
2. For a bluestocking
3. For a suffragette
4. For an actress at the National Theatre
5. For a semi-virgin
6. For a grand lady
7. For a gambler
8. For a minister's lady
9. For a coquette
10. For a flirt
11. For an American
12. For a bar hostess

LA VIE PARISIENNE.

AU BORD DE LA MER

At the seaside

The happiest of the three is not the one who is floating

PARISIAN WOMEN AT THE SEASIDE
"Does the sea air do you good?" "No…it tires me out: my husband doesn't sleep a wink all night."

THE HUSBAND
TRAVELS BY TRAIN:
A FAST-MOVING STORY

1. He leaves alone
2. But there are two in the
   compartment
3. They are attracted to one another
4. Love...
5. But alas, the story comes to an
   end. Back to reality!

1

2

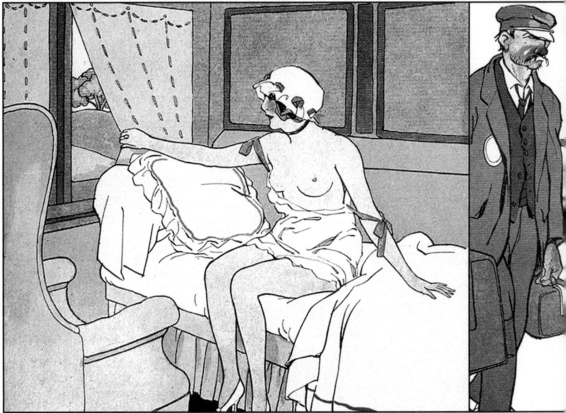

4

5

3

F. Fabiano

PARIS FASHION

"Nudity is always in fashion, but dresses with tails are no longer worn!"

OSTEND, THE MERMAID
When no hearts are available, she devours oysters for lunch

THE NAÏVE CONVENT GIRL

"So much water!... But why has God created such a huge bathtub for the Bretons who never wash!"

WHAT YOUNG GIRLS DREAM ABOUT

"Well, little Line, what are you dreaming about in this beautiful place?

"I'd really like to know if the pearls belonging to that fat lady at the hotel are real!"

Please don't come in yet, I'm not decent. I haven't put on my bathing suit

How Mimi uses a screen, a tub and her Siren bathing suit to experience the seaside without leaving Paris

BATHERS

The wave's first caress

An eclipse of the sun

Only the first step gives you wet feet

Chatting at sea

Gossip on the beach

HOW TO BE A YACHTSMAN

1. First get the kit

2. And a full crew

3. Then the guests

4. And a gypsy band. But don't worry about the yacht. It's not important!

Holidays

A modern Naiad

The most beautiful view in Normandy

Winter
Sports

WINTER SPORTS
Throwing snowballs

The champion skier

On the slopes in Saint-Moritz

HOLIDAY ACTIVITIES
Climbing the Alps

Country
Pursuits

1. **The Neophyte**
   Mad about hunting,
   he was given an old but
   fast horse on graduation,
   and never misses a hunt.

2. **The Poseur**
   He rides badly and knows nothing
   about the hunt but is always
   perfectly turned out. Did he join
   just to be photographed?

3. **The Baron**
   On becoming a millionaire
   he became a baron, and on
   becoming a baron he joined the hunt.
   Huffing and puffing in his too tight
   clothes he rides an old nag that he
   paid much too much for, but nobody
   laughs at him…he's far too rich.

4. **The Social Climber**
   He hunts to meet important
   people and hopes to succeed by
   ingratiating himself with the ladies.
   This strategy has some charm,
   but is also very inconvenient.

5. **The One Who Misses the Boat**
   Noisy, mixing everything up,
   he gives his guests information they
   didn't ask for, and his servants instructions
   they don't understand. He's forgiven
   because he owns some fine woods
   and one needs him, but he'll have
   to wait a very long time for a title.

Two little pigeons for unlucky guns

AMAZONS

1. **The Beginner**
    Knows no fear and gallops like the devil

2. **The Poseur**
    Always first in the saddle, she rarely follows the hunt as she is only interested in her riding habit and hat, which suit her so well

3. **The Galloper**
    Hunts only for the ride, seeks out obstacles, jumps them all and proceeds at a gallop

4. **The Flirt**
    Always rides at walking pace, so convenient for a little romance; she only likes a horse for its rider

5. **The Enthusiast**
    She's a born hunter, always first behind the pack

6. **The Dilettante**
    Where's she got to? One never knows… She suddenly disappears, only to turn up at the château in the evening, somewhat tired. Its so exhausting getting lost in the woods!

The husband: What are you waiting for, Gaston?... What's stopping you?

Gaston: I'm sorry, Sir. I thought she was a protected species.

There is bait to lure and there is alluring bait

Fishing for crayfish

Through
The
Seasons

Spring flowers: Lily of the valley

The first lilacs: help yourselves, gentlemen!

May breezes

The awakening of spring

The swing

The first buds

A botany lesson in the park

Winter is coming: the last swallow

WATCHING THE LEAVES TURN YELLOW

"Shall I succumb to Fernand with his protestations of love?...Shall I fall into the arms of Henri who caresses me with his eyes? ...The doctor was quite right to tell my husband that a stay in the country would do him no good!"

Pets

and their

Mistresses

Monkeys

Japan comes to Paris

Parrots and parakeets

Cats and kittens

The
Soubrette

Mirror, mirror on the wall

Add some white, add some black, add some rouge, Jeannette, men only like the natural look with make-up!

STUDIO SKETCHES
Models at rest

F. Fabiano

"What a strange artist. He spends all his time kissing me while I'm posing."

Girl in a hurry...or an improvised slide

THE SEVEN DEADLY SINS
Envy, Anger, Avarice, Pride, Lust, Sloth, Gluttony

INNOCENT PASTIMES
Dominoes

"You're really lucky to be going to the spa. I can't afford it."

"Don't be silly, you get the money to pay for it by going there."

A love letter

CHANGING ROOM GOSSIP

"You flirt with Pierre, you play the coquette with Paul…What does your husband think of it all?"

"Surely you know that the right hand must never know what the left hand is giving away!"

THE EVOLUTION
OF THE BATHTUB

1. In the Trianon: a clog-shaped bath.
2. 1810: an antique-style tub in
   a Pompeian boudoir.
3. 1830: a crystal bathtub.
4. 1860: a sip of burgundy in
   a lot of water.
5. 1913: The marble bathtub.
6. Tomorrow's fashion:
   the swimming pool.

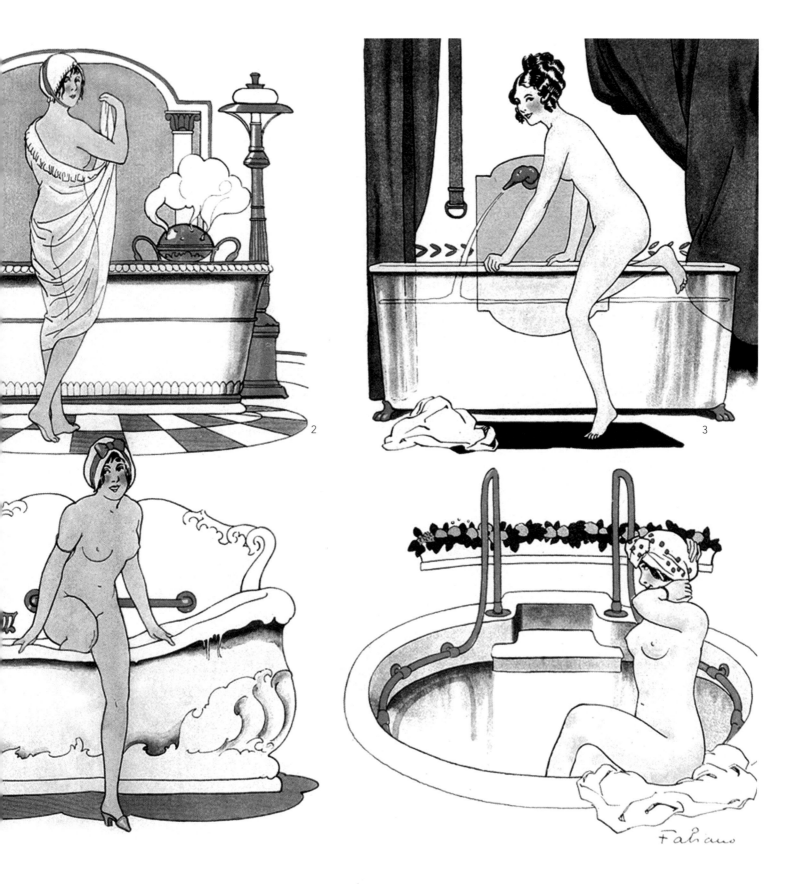

WAKING UP IN PARIS

1. Am I as pretty today as
   I was yesterday?

2. Does Jacques still love me?
   I'm sure he's forgotten to write
   to me.

3. As I thought! His
   aunt is still ill...

4. I'll have my breakfast anyway.
   Musn't let jealousy spoil my
   appetite.

5. I almost forgot my little pet
   under the bed.

6. Now for serious things.
   What shall I wear today?...

F Fabiano

PARISIAN BIRDS
The chick

SYMPHONY IN WHITE MAJOR
The Queen of the washerwomen

PILLOW TALK
Drawing-room secrets

Fabiano

A GOURMET SUPPER

A little bird, fruit and champage. Dinner is served!

Friandises

SWEETMEATS
The neighbour's apples

SECRETS OF THE BOUDOIR
Madame wiles away the day

F. Fabiano

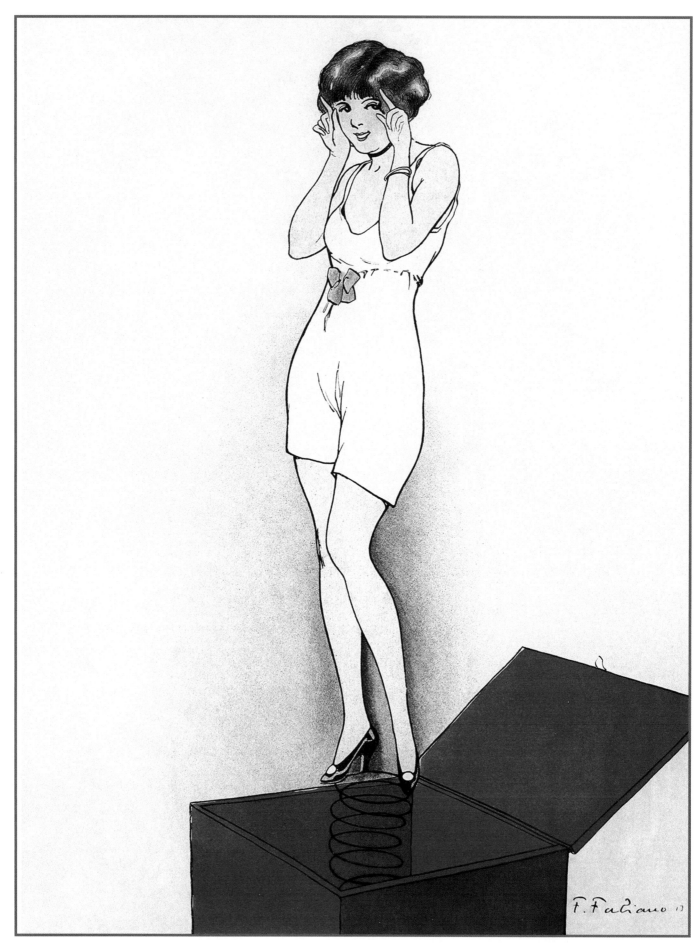

New Year's Day surprise – a naughty Jill-in-a-box

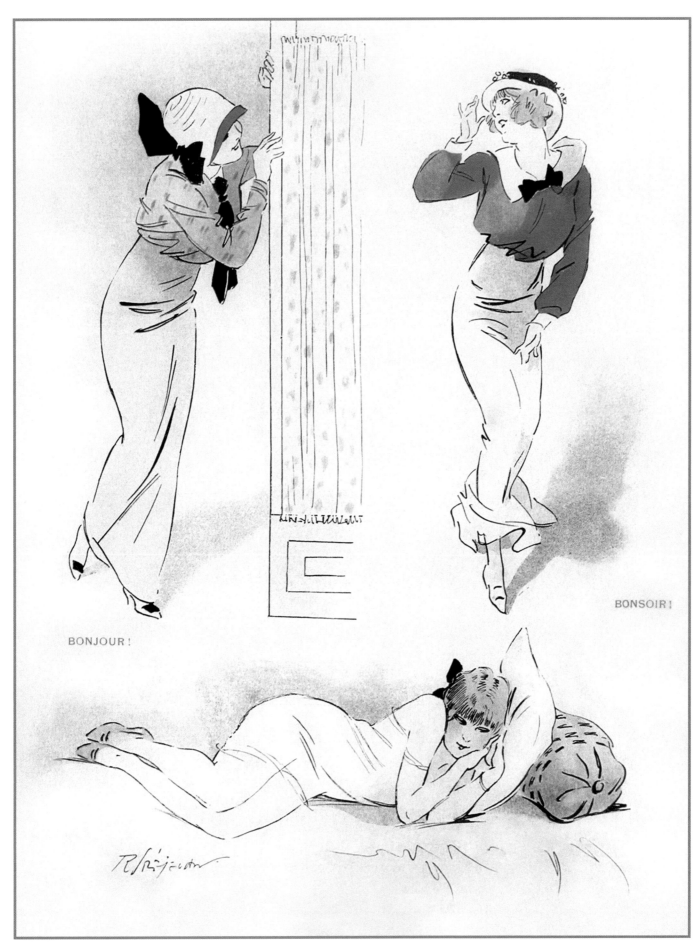

BONJOUR!

BONSOIR!

Good morning! Good night!

Fashion

FABRICS

1. Canvas

4. Muslin

2. Lace

5. Velvet

3. Moiré

6. Linen

The new hat

AUTREFOIS... AUJOURD'HUI...

FASHION AND MANNERS – SIMPLE COMPARISONS

(From the top) *(From the top)*
Then... Nowadays...
1. The dress had to fit perfectly 1. The less coordinated the better
2. Undressing a pretty woman was extraordinarily complicated 2. It takes no time at all
3. The hat provided a harmonious frame for the face 3. It looks like a candle snuffer
4. Fashionable young women were tightly corseted 4. Do you prefer today's excesses?

A love offering

THE FASHION FOR PAINTED STOCKINGS

1. For a literary woman
2. For an engaged woman
3. For the Countess of Posh
4. For a general's wife
5. For a lady of the night
6. For a great lover
7. For a messenger girl
8. For a showgirl

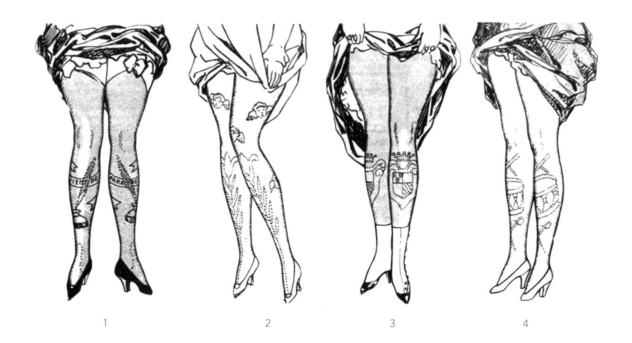

1   2   3   4

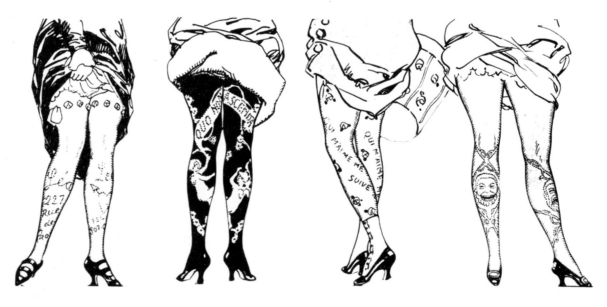

5   6   7   8

The dress with the most beautiful train of all...

LES GIBOULÉES DE LA SAINT-MARTIN IL PLEUT, IL PLEUT, BERGÈRE !...

It's raining, it's raining...

FASHIONABLE COIFFURES:

1. The discreet garden. 2. Cornfield in the wind.

3. Chignon of perpetual snow. 4. Waves of a turbulent sky.

5. The flowering shrub.

STUDIO SKETCHES
Models of all sorts

FASHIONABLE PARASOLS

A Japanese autumn

VENETIAN FASHION COMES TO PARIS

1. Down with the Persian turban, on with the Venetian bonnet

2. Are we threatened with 40 HP gondolas in the streets of Paris?

3. Will drawing-rooms be cluttered with sumptuous dresses with long trains?

4. You don't have to go to Venice to find a pigeon to pluck…

5. Or to be familiar with the bitter-sweet poetry of the Bridge of Sighs!

Was that really Diana's hunting outfit? Its got a nice décolleté, and the skirt is elegant

Men and
Women

Banker, beggar, general or simple soldier, man's destiny is to be a puppet on a string!

At the fashionable portrait painter's studio: "Dear Master, do I really have to strip down to my chemise for you to paint my portrait? My husband told me you were conscientious, but I hadn't realised to what extent."

1.

"I'll be with you at five. I'll be yours…"

2.

What shall I wear? Pyjamas are too intimate

3.

Evening dress is too formal

4.

A dressing gown isn't very elegant

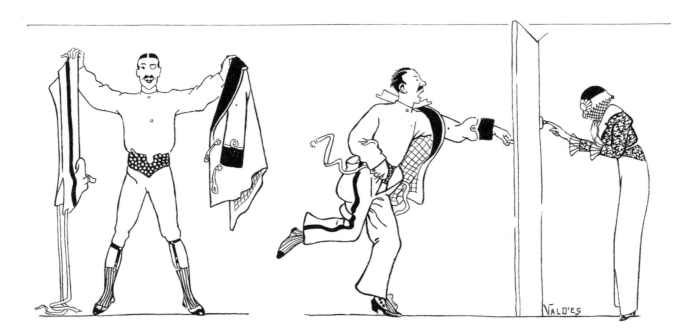

5.

I know! A smoking jacket combines fashion with superb comfort

6.

There's a ring…
Don't come in…
Another ring…
Dammit, it's her…
What will she
think of my
state of undress?

Dreams of the future: "Well, my dear, what would you say to a pretty little house where I could come and visit you three times a week?"

"Three times a week…you're boasting!"

TELEGRAPHIC EXCUSES
"Impossible come this evening. Must stay Paris for official banquet. Love. Henri"
"The monster. It sounds more like an intimate dinner to me!"

A businessman. "What's Jules doing these days?" "Fooling around as usual." "Ah!...That must be why he's telling everyone he's so busy!"

"What's the hound for?"

"I'm afraid of the neighbour: when he flirts with me he goes too far."

"Too far?...You mean he holds you too close!"

LOVE IN PRACTICE

"Since you love him, you silly girl, don't resist. It's only the first step that will cost you!"

"Really? I was told that would be the most profitable!..."

The victim of too placid a husband

"Men, what a breed!"

The victim of too ardent a husband

"You poor dear, stay with us"

Gossip over the fruit and wine

"I really don't understand you. You're unfaithful to Paul, Paul is unfaithful to you, and yet you're the best of friends."

"My dear girl, only those who do nothing are never wronged."

A DIFFICULT CHOICE

"Paul says 'I adore you,' Pierre says 'I love you.' Which shall I choose?"

THE SEVEN DEADLY SINS

1. **Sloth:** Women can be cured of sloth only
   by vanity or love
   (La Bruyère)

2. **Lust:** The most effective mortification
   for lust is abstinence and fasting
   (Buffon)

3. **Avarice:** Poverty lacks many things:
   avarice lacks everything
   (La Bruyère)

4./5. **Gluttony and Envy:**
   Envy is the best sauce for gluttony:
   the neighbour's apples are always the
   most delicious (Saint-Evremond)

6. **Anger:** Of what use is anger without power? (Corneille)

7. **Pride:** Unimportant people take pride in
always talking about themselves; the
great take pride in never doing so
(Voltaire)

"You're really giving up the stage?"
"Yes. I'm told I have star quality but I never get a starring part.

"He said that he loved me, that he adored me, that he would marry me.
If he lies so convincingly he can't be as stupid as he looks!"

"My dear child, I see in your hand that a very wealthy gentleman wants to make your fortune."

"It's true, Madame Memphis, but if I listen to him I'll be called a tart."

"And if you don't listen to him you'll be called a goose. What a difficult decision!"

THE KISS

1. Handsome Pecopin was looking for an adventure

2. A woman passes by…he follows her

3. He declares his love

4. He begs for a kiss

5. He thought he had made a conquest

6. But that kiss cost him a car and a villa in Deauville…
Moral: Illusion is happiness.

Stolen kisses

"You're looking at my pearls?...
They were the first present I ever received and they sealed my fate: a woman's virtue often hangs on a string...of pearls."

"With your fine words and grand phrases, I can see you coming: all you drawing-room moralists are the same!"

"How did you make Paul keep his promises?" "I pointed out that debts of the heart are the only ones that still constitute a criminal offence."

Unity is strength

Modern
Myths

Young girls dream on Christmas Eve

Two idols

Tripping up

Butterflies

SECRETS OF THE RUE DE LA PAIX

A mannequin's story

The School for Sirens

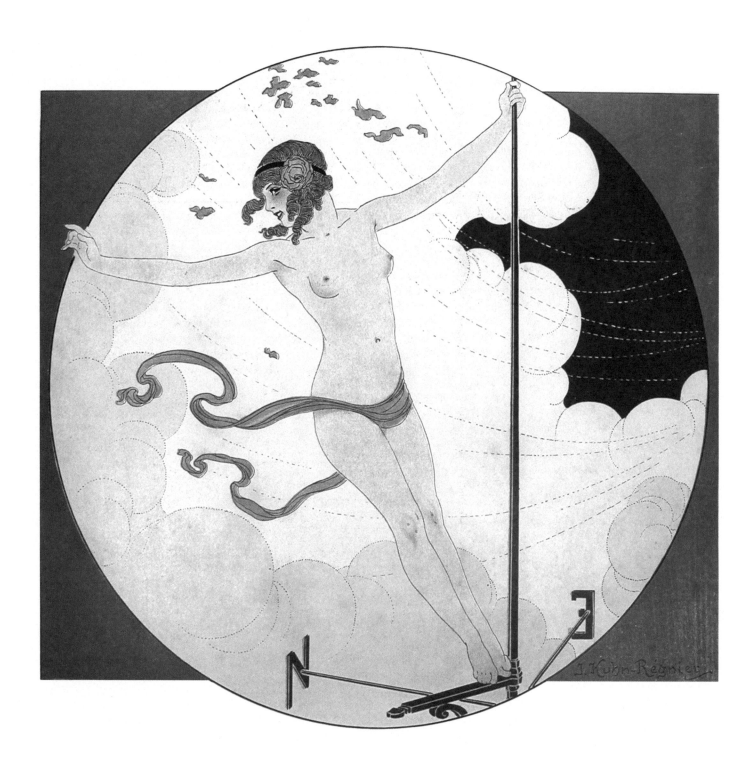

An eternal girouette

The water nymph waiting for her lover

The carriage of an elegant woman in ancient times

The Queen of Thule drains her cup

ANCIENT TIMES, THE BOXER

"I swear by Venus I only want to say one word to him…"

En regardant cette image
Bien des folles souriront ;
Mais peut-être que les sages
En comprendront la leçon...

Car combien de bachelettes
Au pauvre cœur hésitant,
Ont comme cette coquette
Une âme de Buridan !

Which one will win her heart?

Theatre and Literature

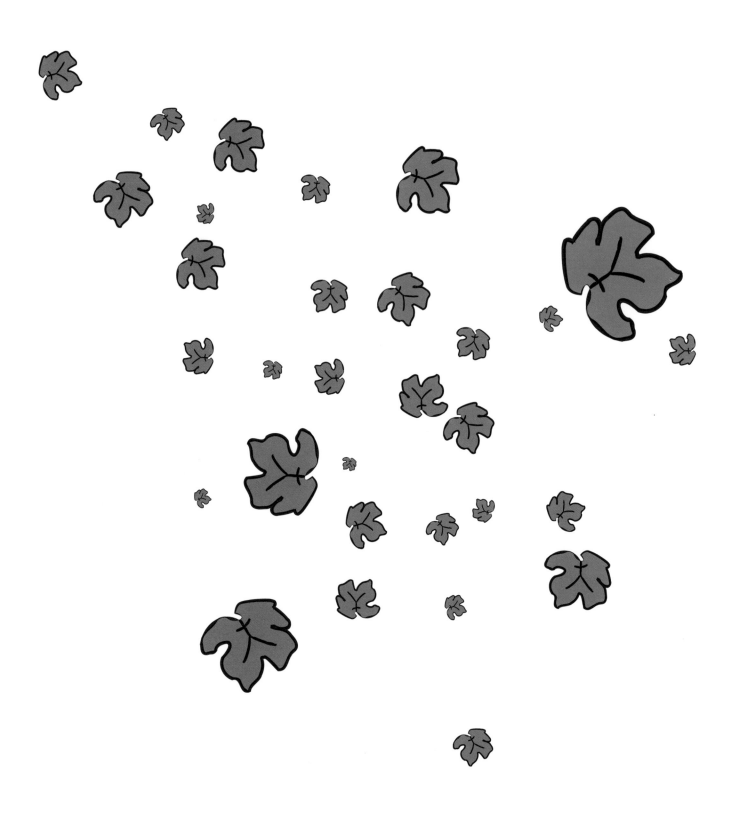

THE NEW TURKEY
The pretty Sultana – the whole of Europe wants to see her dance!

FASHION YESTERDAY AND TODAY
The tango they danced in in the drawing rooms of Pompeii!

The dance of the wind and the sea

The Ballets Russes

The ballet of the Thousand and One Nights

BC: Dance in the days of the pharaohs

The Ballet of the Rose Queen

A SHORT HISTORY OF THE THEATRE

1. Greek drama

2. Romantic drama

3. Persian drama

4. 18th century romantic drama

5. Romantic drama in the 20th century

"Gentlemen, turn the page quickly!..If a poor young lady has lost her shoe in
the middle of *La Vie Parisienne*, there's no reason for her to lose her reputation as well…"

The eternal comedy of Paris fashion

Everyone who's anyone has arrived...we can raise the curtain

1. Lord Plumcake has come to Paris to see the Parisian girls, but is disappointed to hear only Spanish in the cafés of Montmartre…

2. He hears only Italian, Romanian and Portuguese on the boulevards…

3. There are only Americans in the Bois de Boulogne…

4. On the Champs Elysées he's addressed in German…

5. At last a young woman addresses him in French: "Would you like to come home with me Monsieur?" Damnation, she's Belgian.